A Handbook for People with Disabilities

NAVIGATING *in the* DARK

PERSONAL STORIES AND TECHNIQUES FOR
OVERCOMING CHALLENGES AND SAYING YES TO LIFE

GIULIA JARAMILLO. MS, LMFT

FLOWER *of* LIFE PRESS

FLOWER OF LIFE PRESS
Voices of Transformation

Are You Ready To Be A Published Author?

Books are the best business card you can have, whether you are an entrepreneur building your company, or a changemaker with a message that needs to be heard. Flower of Life Press is committed to giving voice to authors—and offering the support that is critical to birthing an authentic and powerful book.

We are ready to serve you with writing coaching, editing, and designwhile we provide the marketing team that will propel your journey and electrify your audience!

Check us out now at **floweroflifepress.com**—and have your book published by the team with over 3,000 books to their credit!

Navigating in the Dark: Personal Stories and Techniques for Overcoming Challenges and Saying Yes to Life

Copyright © 2019 Giulia Jaramillo

All rights reserved. No part of this publication may be reproduced, distributed, or transmitted in any form or by any means, including photocopying, recording, or other electronic or mechanical methods, without the prior written permission of the publisher, except in the case of brief quotations embodied in critical reviews and certain other noncommercial uses permitted by copyright law.

The content of this book is for general instruction only. Each person's physical, emotional, and spiritual condition is unique. The instruction in this book is not intended to replace or interrupt the reader's relationship with a physician or other mental health professional. Please consult your doctor for matters pertaining to your specific health.

Book design by Jane Ashley, floweroflifepress.com

To contact the publisher, visit floweroflifepress.com

Library of Congress Control Number: Available upon request.

ISBN-13: 978-1-7337409-4-4

Printed in the United States of America

"In the stillness of your own presence, you can feel your own formless and timeless reality as the unmanifested life that animates in your physical form. You can then feel the same life deep within every other human and every other creature. You look beyond the veil of form and separation. This is the realization of oneness. This is love."

—ECKHART TOLLE

Praise for Giulia's Work

As a visual artist I have always believed in the saying, "A picture is worth a thousand words", but after meeting Giulia my mind has changed. She has a wonderful gift. Like trying to put a puzzle together without a reference picture, she can take your thousand words, put them together and show you the true picture. She sees what cannot be visually seen. It's as if the vision we take for granted has become our handicap, not being able to see the forest from the trees. But with her guidance you will not be lost in the foreboding woods but brought to the path of enlightenment.

—G. HARRIS SPICER

After the devastating loss of my husband, I felt lost and heartbroken. I thought I would never feel normal again. Giulia helped me sort through my emotions and learn how to grieve. She was a savior during my time of need and I wholeheartedly recommend her to anyone I can. She is amazing in her field and her sincerity is unmatched. I owe her more than I could ever say.

—CYNTHIA O'BRIAN

I first met Giulia about 15 years ago at a Kinesiology class that we were both attending. I looked around the room, looking for a place to sit—one that would accommodate my short legs. I am not sure who said "Hello" first. I do remember Giulia saying to me, with a laugh, that if I was looking for a seat that was comfy where my feet would reach the floor, I should come sit with her on the love-seat. Seems she had already checked out all of the possible seating! In that minute, a friendship was born. Giulia is warm, loving, and generous to a fault. She is also very funny, a bit outspoken, opinionated, determined, and passionate about her family, her friends, and her career. As a Therapist, she excels. I had no idea that Macular Degeneration was a part of her life that first day. She had told me her husband had dropped her off and would be picking her up. I offered to drive her home, since we are basically neighbors. She said that would be great! After that, I would pick her up every weekend. It never occurred to me to ask her to drive. Our friendship is one of mutual trust, love, and dependency. I read menus to her; she leads me to my car in the dark. Yes, she sees much better in the dark than I do! As a friend, she is loyal, fiercely protective, and as giving of her time as she can be. Her family very much comes first. Not just her husband and her two boys. Family is her Mom, her brothers, her nieces... They are priority. The spelling of her name "Giulia" is very indicative of the lady that she is. Lovely, graceful, charming, sincere. And just a bit mysterious!

—CHRIS, CT.

I moved to Connecticut after dealing with some life-changing medical issues. I was lost and, being a firm believer in therapy, sought someone who could help me "find my way again". I was given Giulia's name and number and I called that day...best decision I have made in years. Her approach to therapy is a perfect match for my needs. She listens. We talk—sometimes I have a planned agenda, sometimes not. She is very good at helping me focus the many ping-pong balls in my mind. She allows me to explore my own instincts and provides valuable guidance that has helped me find my own path. She does not dwell on diagnosis and clinical theories but instead the now...how does what I am feeling affect me now and how will my actions make me feel later. She also has no problem cutting through my own defense mechanisms and she laughs at the very random things I sometimes bring up.

I trust her completely.

—TODD L., CT.

Giulia has worked her magic on my anxiety more times than I can even mention here. She has a sixth sense that amazes many of us who know her. She is a feisty fighter who has overcome obstacles most would have just given up on long ago. Giulia has a calming way and a sense of humor that puts you immediately at ease.

—RAVEN

Giulia's guidance speaks truth and her compassion behind it sees no end. Her devotion to her work reaches volumes, and her originality is untouched. When I think about when I first walked into her office, I was a girl who was so lost, and I lacked so much self-worth. I saw no light within my journey in life. Meeting Giulia, I found my safe place. She carries an energy about her that allows you to be able to fully open without even trying. Her capacity to understand while allowing her wisdom to reach, gives perspective and hope. I'm very grateful for Giulia and her teachings. She was the light within my dark tunnel. She sparked the dim light I had within and now I know how to shine on my own again. I owe her so much.

—ALEISHA C., CT.

I first sat down with Giulia over two years ago to have our first conversation. She informed me of her Macular Degeneration and how it would not impact our sessions. I can attest that this has remained true, and that her level of intellect and abilities altogether has exceeded any expectation I had from her. I was impressed by her brainpower and her ability to grasp qualities about me that I had been unable to recognize on my own. Giulia is consistently learning, researching and applying her findings to our sessions to assist in improving my emotional, spiritual and physical health. I have greatly treasured her insight to me as an individual and am confident that I will continue to be graced with her skill-set throughout my life.

—ALLISON M. HAYES

Note from Giulia

The best praise I could've gotten by far is this letter from my niece Olivia. This was written as a school assignment for her fifth-grade class—the kids were asked to write an essay about their hero:

My hero doesn't wear a cape or has special vision. Every day she pushes me to the limit even though I hardly see her. My hero is my Zia Zia. Zia Zia is Italian for aunt. If you don't know, my Zia Zia is legally blind. Even though she is blind, she is still my favorite. One of my favorite moments is every year she brings my sister and me to downtown Westerly. We go get new Vera Bradley backpacks, fudge, and go to whatever shops I want to go to. My Zia Zia taught me how to cook and bake. I really wish I could have those anchelatis right now! I know you can't see that well, but you still bring me back items from when you go on vacations. And also, you still write a birthday card to me and my sister every year. You work a lot being a psychologist and trying to get place to place. Almost every year I get to go in your pool and sleep over even though you are super busy. You always nurture me when something goes wrong even though you have had it. My Zia Zia always compliments me and my family. Usually she calls me every month just to check in on my grades and how I am doing. Zia Zia, I know you can't see well but I hope you can see clearly that I love you.

—OLIVIA

GIULIA AND HER SONS, LUCAS AND JACOB

DEDICATION

I dedicate this book to my husband Daniel and our sons Jacob and Lucas.

Without each of you I would have never been able to accomplish all that I have in my life.

I love each of you with each and every breath, and with all of my heart and soul.

Thank you for being you.

Contents

Note from the Publisher *by Scott Watrous* xv
Definition of "Being Disabled" xix
Preface xxi

The 8 Practices: An Overview 1
Self-contract 5
Personal Daily Inventory 7
Introduction 13
Practice #1: Honesty is the Best Policy 19
Practice #2: Let Go and Forgive 33
Practice #3: Trust Your Body Wisdom 41
Practice #4: Build Your Self-Confidence 51
Practice #5: Stand Up for Yourself,
Speak Your Truth, and Find Your Power 59
Practice #6: Create Healthy Relationships 71
Practice #7: Use Humor and Laugh
through Your Pain 83
Practice #8: Honesty is the Best Policy 89

Afterword 101
Acknowledgments 107
About the Author 113
Resources 114

Note from the Publisher

by Scott Watrous

I've met a huge number of authors over the 35 years I've been in the book business: famous politicians and pundits, literary stars, health and wellness experts... writers of all walks of life have crossed my path—even Dr. Seuss, who signed *The Cat in the Hat* for me! I've been blessed to spend a big part of my life supporting brave men and women with stories to tell and wisdom to share—yet none of them shine as brightly in my memory as Giulia Jaramillo.

The book in your hands is many things, first an autobiography of a very special woman—and through that story, a guidebook to living life with the disability of Macular Degeneration—or any disability. Surrounded by secrets and shame, Giulia survived the deep challenges of a broken family, and the seemingly impossible task of navigating in the darkness that surrounded her. At once shocking and triumphant, this story of courage, perseverance and heart grabs your attention, wakes you up, and offers hope for all of us.

Sitting across from Giulia for the first time in her office, I experienced firsthand the conundrum of "disability"—what the body shows the world is not an accurate reflection of a person. She is, in her own words, "blind as a bat", yet her "vision" is well beyond 20/20. Within her petite frame resides a fearlessness born of a lifetime of struggle, and a positivity that permeates her every action. She is really funny, and fun to be with, yet I can't help but feel the pain she has suffered on her long journey up until now. Listening to her tell stories is a wild ride, each one ripe with the deep pain of dis-ease, and the joy of succeeding when the odds are stacked against her.

Giulia is the personification of resilience—and I marvel at the courage that this woman drew upon throughout her life, and what a gift she must be to her patients. What better therapist could there be than one who has lived through hell and come out the other side? This book is for those broken by dis-ease, of course...but her message is way bigger than that. If you are human, you will connect with Giulia's struggle, and see facets of your life in hers.

I am proud to know Giulia Jaramillo and honored to be part of giving her voice a place to resonate.

Definition of "Being Disabled"

For the purpose of this book, the definition of being disabled by this author is:

Anyone who struggles with limited vision, limited hearing, blindness, deafness, loss of a limb or body part, Bipolar I, Bipolar II, Trauma PTSD, Schizophrenia, Schizo-affective Disorder, Panic Disorder, Major Depressive Disorder, ADHD, ADD, Substance Abuse, Autism, and Dementia.

If we look deep inside, we all have something that we struggle with. The level of the struggle can leave us limited in our capacity to fulfill the activities of daily life. However, regardless of their limitation, NO ONE is unworthy of kindness, respect, justice and fairness in their life. No disability should be the cause for anyone's rights to be compromised.

Preface

I wrote this book for anyone who is struggling and feeling alone and confused by their disability and its impact on their life. I've shared deeply painful parts of my story so that you can see that you, in fact, are NOT alone. You CAN find new ways of facing your challenges, and you CAN persevere and come back to create a life full of meaning and joy. Heck, if I can do it, ANYONE can! Just because you have a disability does NOT make you unworthy! You are inherently worthy of love, safety, laughter, joy, and honesty. No matter what anyone says, THIS is the truth, my friend. So read on...

I hope the words that I have shared in this book help anyone who is considered limited in some way. The world has room for all of us no matter what capacities we have or do not have. It is what we do with all that we have that matters. We can do anything we can set our minds to. A fulfilling life is 99% effort! Get to know yourself and then take charge of how you want your world to be. *You are the only one that can make the decisions and choices to get there.*

Trust your voice! Remember, people like to stay inside their own comfort zone, so people with differences and new ways of doing things usually make people uncomfortable. Do not give in to the discomfort—let it be your driving force. Stand up for YOU! Do not let fear stop you.

Do what you must do to get your needs met. As long as you are not hurting anyone or yourself then there is no reason for you to *not* take action. Let the force of courage and conviction be your guide and let it always be with you.

Each of the 8 Practices in this book features some of my own story, as well as tools that will help you understand and gain insight into your own journey, and how you can navigate in the darkness of your disability.

Disabled people have very few chances to be seen for who they really are, because other people tend to see us as broken at first, and will sometimes shroud our voices with their judgments. If you have a special person with whom you can be truly open and expressive with, great. If not, a journal can be your best friend! I couldn't have survived without mine. By recording your thoughts and dreams somewhere, you are empowering yourself to create the life you want. I always wrote on paper—but an iPad or a voice memo will also do the job. Whatever works for you. Remember: Be honest with yourself. Your journal is a place for your truth to be honored.

Embrace all of your life experiences, because now is the time to learn the lessons and cultivate gratitude for all of it. This path is about overcoming and moving into a place of positivity in your life. The Universe will keep trying to get your attention unless you stay present with the pain and learn to re-pattern it! By examining your life through the eyes of the 8 Practices, each day will offer a challenge *and* an opportunity to live your truth. This is your daily practice.

Before you dive right in, please read the 8 Practices below, and then sign the Self-Contract. This is your chance to really commit to changing the way you relate to your world so you can discover a new level of joy and contentedness. So please sign the thing and let's do this!

The 8 Practices: An Overview

1. **Be honest with yourself & face your truth:** Even if Ben Franklin said it first, it's always been right and continues to be. The more honesty you have in your life, the less weight you have to carry around on your shoulders, and the more you will trust yourself and your life path.

2. **Let go and forgive:** People do not know what it is like to be you, so let go of anger and victim energy. Holding onto it only hurts YOU and keeps your relationships from flourishing. Don't hold a grudge or be bitter—these energies are toxic to your system.

3. **Trust your body wisdom:** Your body wisdom will guide you in the right direction. Have patience and practice listening deeply to that internal knowing so you can hear what your body is telling you.

4. **Build your self-confidence:** Concentrate on your strengths instead of your weaknesses. In my case, my brain was my strength, and I used it every way I could so that I wouldn't focus on the fact that I really couldn't see a heck of a lot going on around me!

5. **Stand up for yourself, speak your truth, and find your power:** You might feel fear while you are speaking up but it is a natural part of the process of becoming empowered. Do not be driven by fear, but instead let it guide you towards what needs to happen for the greater good. No one can create your life but you. No one can show your potential but you. This may mean you have to say "NO" sometimes or set a boundary with a family member, a friend, or a college roommate. You have to stand tall in your truth and be willing to act accordingly. Be YOU. Know YOU. What's the message that your mind, body and spirit are delivering to you?

6. **Be kind and helpful:** Keep your heart open, respect other people, and have a service-oriented mindset. Show up for others and find ways to be in service. If the people who have wronged you ever need you, show up for them anyway. There is freedom in getting out of your own story and focusing on being in service to others.

7. **Use humor and laugh through the pain:** Find the ability to laugh at yourself! Find the humor in the pain, otherwise you'll only wallow and suffer endlessly. Laughter is the fastest way to shift your mood and create a positive vibration for you and those around you. It's also a doorway into joy, and the world needs a lot more of that! Do not be afraid of laughing *at*

yourself. I have found it to be the best medicine. I laugh and then I use a coping skill along with it to correct and/or create what is needed.

8. **Don't take anything personally:** Hey, we don't know what we don't know, right? *Forgiveness* is key here, and also *surrender*. When you can take the high road, then you will avoid unnecessary whacks to your self-esteem and be able to sustain your relationships, protect your soul, and your integrity. You must keep your boundaries and remember that other people's judgments are false. They will never be able to understand your capacities, and you MUST keep your reaction to that under control, so you don't get lost in anger. You have to be your own driving force. Whatever is true for YOU, is what you need to trust. Follow your inner guidance and allow that strength from within to emerge. If you're looking outside of yourself for answers or saving, you'll likely be disappointed and won't reach your goals.

Self-Contract

Please read and sign below:

I, _____
agree to uphold these 8 Practices and truths to the best of my ability. I agree to remember these truths, act on them in each moment, and apply them to my relationships and daily life.

Sign_____

Date_____

Personal Daily Inventory

One practice that will really help you is called **Blink, breathe, and filter.** *Blink* means to stop and gather your thoughts by focusing on your blinking. This will help you ground yourself. *Breathe* means to take a deep breath and hold for the count of three at the top before letting your breath out. The exhale should be as slow as possible. Do it for at least 3 times (it will feel like forever but it actually happens really quickly). *Filter* means to think about what is happening. Think about what is the highest and best choice for the situation in that moment. What is the result you are looking to achieve at that time?

Take an inventory of your life at the end of each day by answering the following questions. Write down your answers in a journal or use a voice recording app on your phone to capture your insights.

1. Were you able to implement any of the 8 Practices? Which ones did you use? Which ones didn't you use?

2. Did you implement the *Blink, breathe, and filter* exercise?

3. What purpose did this conversation serve for you?

4. What purpose did this conversation serve for the other person? (If you do not know this answer it is imperative that you find out.)

5. Did you ask questions such as "please help me to understand" or "I just want to be clear prior to answering you or going any further"? Understand and meet the person where they are in their mindset. If not, the end result will probably not be positive.

6. Did you answer a question with a question? Until you are clear on what is being asked, it is best not to answer but to keep asking questions for clarity. This technique will buy you some time and will help you get clear on what is going on and what is needed.

7. Were you able to stay in the moment? The only thing we have is the now. Remembering to stay in the moment and not bringing up past or future topics will keep the conversation flowing smoothly.

8. Did you respond in an impulsive or emotional matter?

9. Were you able to clearly express your thoughts? (Remember, you can always buy time if you state that you will get back to them at a later date.)

10. Did you have a conversation while you were angry? This should never occur. Anger is a secondary emotion NOT a primary emotion. It is important that you reason out what the anger is about before engaging anyone. Where is it coming from and what main emotion is being triggered? Two main emotions are passion and pain, and these emotions can be felt at the same time or separately. So first, reason out if you are mad, sad, or indifferent. Then, identify what are facts and what are non-facts. Attempt to stick to the facts at all times. This doesn't mean that you need to be a robot and *not* feel emotions. In fact, your emotions serve a very important role in getting your needs met! However, if you are reactive rather than responsive, and not coming from a place of unconditional regard and empathy, you may encounter problems. So identify where the emotion is coming from and how it is helping you in the moment.

11. Did you consider what was highest and best for you in the situation? Sometimes we become fixated on achieving our goals and objectives that we are not able to make wise choices in the moment. What is that moment calling for? What direction is the situation going? Is it a good time or not? Do you need to retreat in order to achieve the best end result for you? Did you need to take the lower position in order to achieve the best goal? Try not to let your ego dictate your thoughts and behaviors. This takes practice but it can be done!

12. Were you the best you could be? Were you true to yourself and your own truth?

13. Were you fair and non-judgmental? Remember, judgment is NOT part of anyone's job, ever.

Introduction

Words echo within me, as if I am in a cave—ugly and painful—like razors bouncing off the walls again and again, drawing blood even now, so many years later...

Stupid
Lazy
Worthless
Not in reality
Not facing the facts
Retarded
A troublemaker
Someone who always defies the rules
Someone who always rocks the boat
Defiant
Stubborn
A cripple
An embarrassment

Looking back, the words meant less than the people saying them. Mom and Dad taught me those words to describe their little girl. They showed me their power over others, and they cut me down at every opportunity...one step forward, two cuts back—every day. They were following what their culture dictated and believed that each of their children had to be born perfect, or else there was something wrong with them as parents. They had to protect themselves by keeping my poor vision a secret—but I was not having it. None of it made sense to me so I tried to listen but I mostly did what I wanted. My strong will would inevitably lead me to be the receiver of the name calling and other destructive behaviors.

Relentless. Destructive. Angry. Ashamed. That could have been me, but it's not. Instead, I removed those negative emotions and replaced them with knowledge and compassion. The lineage of rage, abuse, and struggle that defined my family system was not me. I refused to judge others the way they judged me, so I was able to break the chain of pain—and for that I am proud and thankful.

My story isn't easy to tell, and it may be hard to hear. All I ask is that you open your heart and remember that this *really* is a happy story. It's funny! I learned long ago that humor makes it easier to be me. Seriously, if you can't laugh at my story, you will cry...and remember that this is a story of *strength and resilience,* and it has an awesome ending!

So let's start with what my life is like now.

Pretend you are walking into my office...

INTRODUCTION

The sign on the door says "Giulia Jaramillo, MS, LMFT". I am sitting behind my desk, and you might be surprised when I get off my chair to greet you. I am not even 5 feet tall! 4 foot 9 to be exact. My brother calls me "two by two". I think that's hysterical! I think I get shorter when my feet touch the ground!

I am round and kind of chubby, I guess, and you won't believe how funny my voice is! When people enter my energy for the first time, they smile and sometimes will say, "Hey, you're short!" I thank them for pointing it out to me. I think that's a great way to start, actually. They are being themselves and saying what is on their mind. Hurray! It usually gets us to laugh. And I get a laugh out of them, so what better way to start the therapeutic relationship!

"Please take a seat, Emelia. I'll hop back up on my chair and then we can start," I say. At that point, I begin to wonder what will give it away to my client...

My clunky electronics that they don't recognize? My CCTV, the talking computer, my computer screen that is really big, with extra-large print? Maybe I'll let them in on my secret right at the start. Whatever feels easiest, since they will likely figure it out pretty soon.

No matter how many times I repeat my story, I still feel a pit at the bottom of my stomach—each and every time I speak the words, "I am legally blind: I have Macular Degeneration. I have had it from birth. So if it seems like I am not looking at you, or not paying attention, I really am. My eyes will shift, but I am always with you, listening and paying attention." This puts the client at ease. However, I am well aware that this is not what the therapy world recommendations, as I have learned through many years of experience.

As students in graduate school for psychotherapy, we were instructed never to disclose anything personal about ourselves to our patients. Yet, here I am breaking that rule—because it is in the best interest of my client. I feel that it is information that, if not discussed, will make the client uncomfortable and uncertain of my capacities as their treatment provider.

One short impactful story...

When I was 13 years old, I decided I was not going to take the abuse anymore. My father physically beat up the family every chance he had—but my mother's verbal abuse hurt me even more than dad's hands. Holidays were the worst, and my brother and I never had a happy one. My father did not believe in celebrating anything, and he made sure we were as unhappy as he was. We knew we would all receive a beating either the day be-

INTRODUCTION

fore or after the Big Day. *One Easter Eve he beat us all so badly that we were all passed out on the floor. When I was able to open my eyes, I saw my father washing his hands and smiling. He then began wiping his fingers, carefully—one at a time, proud of their prowess at beating his children and wife. He looked at me slowly, eyes flat and hollow, and put a finger to his lips as if to say, "Don't speak if you know what's good for you". I closed my eyes and cried silently.*

You're probably thinking, "How awful!" or "What horror!" right?

Yes...*and*...it's okay to take a breath. Inhale, exhale, repeat.

As awful as it was, it was another lesson for me.

So here's what I know now:

Life is a fusion of humor and tragedy.

Without laughter, the tragedy of my life would have completely overwhelmed me. So if you can read on and take this journey with me I hope the stories and the words will help you in some way.

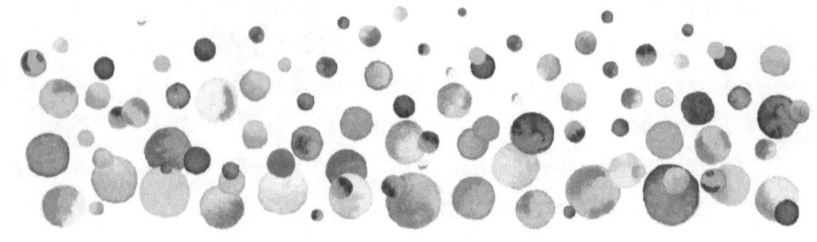

I release all drama from my life.

PRACTICE #1

Be Honest With Yourself and Face Your Truth

"Honesty is the best policy." Even if Ben Franklin said it first, this statement has always been right and continues to be. The more honesty you have in your life, the less baggage you have to carry around on your shoulders.

My life has two very distinct parts: dark stories and struggle before the secret was revealed, and then—like a thunder-clap—at age 35 my life began anew. In one moment, *everything shifted in my life*. With one question, the huge house of lies that my parents built began to crumble, and I saw for the first time just how much suffering I went through to protect my parents and their deep shame.

THE BIG REVEAL

I was born partially blind, and my vision continued to get worse. When I started having bigger problems with my vision at age 10, my parents were instructed to take me up to Boston General Eye and Ear Hospital. But they weren't having it. They told me that Boston was too much of a commute and that they would take me to a specialist in Providence, Rhode Island instead. Since my father was not comfortable driving long distances, one of my cousins was asked to come along so that they would be able to learn the way and then my father would be able to drive me himself. My father took me several times after the initial visit. One day, he came to me and told me that I would need to find myself a ride if I wanted to continue going to these visits. He could not afford to miss any more work.

It was a terrible feeling...I felt like such a burden to the family. I spent lots of time trying to get someone to drive me. No one I knew could help. Finally, I called the local Red Cross. They had volunteers that did this type of work. So each time I had another doctor's appointment I called again, and they transported me. I was so afraid, but I was more afraid of not going and not getting to the bottom of my vision problems.

I kept saying to myself, "If only I could see!" I hated myself for causing all of my family's problems. After my first few visits, the doctor told me that there was nothing they could do to help me, assuring me I was never "going to go black," but that my vision was inevitably going to get worse.

When I told my mother, she said, "You should have died when you were born." I was nothing but another cross to bear in her life.

And then, in her extra-evil voice, she told me to not ever say anything to anyone about my vision problems—anyone!—because she needed to get me married off. She was *not* going to be stuck with her spinster daughter for the rest of her life. The look in her eye was so menacing that I can still see it in my mind to this day.

I couldn't stop crying for days on end. I was alone in this; I was never going to be taken care of. I felt the hole it burned in my heart and soul. It was my day of awakening—my new reality. It was also the day a part of me died, too. My inner child had to grow up. So, I would spend the rest of my days pretending I was dumb. I navigated in the dark rather than speaking the truth about my vision problems.

Finally, after years of shame, guilt and humiliation from playing pretend and trying to please others, I stopped living the lie and took control of my destiny. I was 35-years old.

On the day I decided to finally go to Boston General Eye and Ear Hospital of my own volition, my life changed. Boston Eye and Ear is the best facility to help people with vision problems. I spent the entire day there and was given genetic testing as well as many vision and blood tests. I was so hopeful and excited all day, feeling like these people could help me, or at least help me understand more about my disability. However, it did not quite work out that way. After 8 hours of testing, I received some shocking news! It was nothing I could have ever imagined...

At the end of the day I met with the head doctor and his team. The first thing the doctor asked me was if my parents were "first cousins or brother and sister". I was confused at first and asked him if he was talking to the wrong patient! After he convinced me otherwise, I asked, "What does that have to do with my eyes, anyway?" Then the doctor proceeded to explain to me what the genetic tests had shown him.

My head was swimming, my heart thumping like crazy... First cousins or brother and sister? What!?

At one point, I remembered hearing my parents talk about how they were distant cousins, but I had thought nothing of it at the time. This doctor was explaining that they were, in fact, either first cousins or brother and sister—and that is why I was born with Macular Degeneration.

PRACTICE #1: BE HONEST WITH YOURSELF AND FACE YOUR TRUTH

(Here comes the *thunder-clap* I referred to at the start of this chapter...)

BOOM! It felt like I'd been hit by lightning and that the world I had known was gone in a flash, suddenly and with no warning!

I cried buckets of tears, and I wanted to throw up. The doctor knew what this meant to me, and how the lies I had been told all my life had just become clear. He suggested that I face my parents, confront them with the truth, and not let this deception destroy me. He told me I scored very high on the psyche testing and to not to let my natural talent go to waste because I had "such" parents.

The next day after I got home, I decided to call my aunt—my mother's sister. I knew that she would tell me the truth, and, well, that she did. She helped complete the story. *I finally* knew the entire story—the real truth.

On the day that I was born, the doctors told my parents that the veins in my eyes were smaller than usual: therefore, I would not have good vision. My scared father didn't want any suspicion about me, or how he and my mother might be related, or anything about having a "crippled child", so he made it very clear to my mother that she was *not to ever tell anyone that they had a child that was less than perfect*. He also demanded that of my aunt.

I can still hear his voice, speaking old-style Italian, of course, something like, "No one must ever know of this—I demand it!"—and that was it. No one ever said a word...at least not to me.

My father was very powerful in the town and reportedly everyone was afraid of him, so no one ever questioned or defied him in any way. No one ever spoke of it again.

My aunt, though, had my back. She apologized to me and told me how badly they all felt that I was stuck with such awful parents.

So the big secret was out, and it explained so many of the things that had been utterly confusing to me all my life. Why wouldn't my parents bring me to the eye doctor? How could my parents have never come to school to defend me all the times my teachers flipped out because they knew I could not see the blackboard—and I never admitted it?

The teachers called me a liar many times and said I was doing it to seek attention. But I don't blame them—it was not their fault. After all, they didn't know the truth, either.

After I talked to my aunt, I went right over to my parents to tell them about what I had learned at the hospital in Boston. My father sheepishly confessed and then told

PRACTICE #1: BE HONEST WITH YOURSELF AND FACE YOUR TRUTH

me that the reason he did not tell me was because he did not want me to hate him. My mother, in typical fashion, totally denied it. She insisted that she never knew and gave me the innocent look I knew so well. I was so angry at her that steam was coming out of my ears! I couldn't believe what I was hearing! My father then turned his anger toward my mother, and said to her, "Shut up and face it!"

The betrayal and pain was unbearable, and to this day I wonder how any parent could do that to a child. As a daughter, I felt one way: emotional. But as a psychotherapist, I knew there was another way—the logical way—and after thirty-five years of lies, I had to trust my heart, and stop listening to my mind. I'm so glad I did.

This was the beginning my new life. My past life had been based on a web of lies. None of it made any sense. How could this be my reality? Who and what could I trust in my life? It looked like the answer was no one and no thing. How could they watch me struggle so much and not step in? How could they step back and punish me so many times for things that they knew I had no control over?

So, I finally knew the truth. My journey was just beginning, and it was time to face it with courage.

As a therapist, I love my patients. It always amazes me, even after all that I have accomplished, that I am the one on this side of the desk. Mama Mia! Just another smidgen of irony—and one of the reasons this life can be so juicy and fun! Who could have guessed my journey would have led to this? *Hmmmm...*

My patients don't all know my story, but everything I know as a therapist comes from my personal experiences growing up—a girl mostly lost in a fog of fear and utter anxiety, struggling to find her voice and purpose. After years of fighting just to be seen and heard, here I am, perched on my chair, waiting for women, men, and children who want *me* to help them! I am so thankful; no words can describe the joy I experience by helping others.

My patients come in all shapes and sizes, each a unique puzzle, yet...once the stories are told and the tears shed, we're all facing the same challenges and skirting the same shadows. Infinite problems, but only one answer: Love. And empathy, compassion, forgiveness, and more love. It sounds so simple, doesn't it?

Today I'm meeting a new patient, and I'm ready to go. I feel a whiff of excitement because I get to help someone start over! Whatever her story is, she is here because she

PRACTICE #1: BE HONEST WITH YOURSELF AND FACE YOUR TRUTH

has the courage to ask for help, and it's time to do the job I love, and to listen...

It's 2pm when Emelia walks in to my office. "Have a seat, Emelia," I say. "Tell me why you're here."

"Well, my life has been pretty confusing, and in the last few years, I've started to try to figure out what's wrong with me and why I'm so unhappy," Emelia responded.

Over the next forty minutes, Emelia told me the story of growing up, feeling unloved, and never fitting in to the family in the same way that her friends seemed to with their families. Her mom was angry, and she didn't know why. Her father drank enough every night to pass out on the couch. No one ever helped her understand anything, and she knew there were secrets that were being kept from her. Her various aunts and uncles always avoided any questions when she asked about the family.

"About a month ago, I did a really bad thing: I went looking through my mother's filing cabinet, cracked it open with a butter knife and what I found threw me for such a loop that I actually thought about killing myself. Because I realized everyone was lying to me about who I was my entire life."

This is an example of how the universe brings people together for a reason. And that everything that happens is part of a divine plan. I know and trust that I am the right person to be Emelia's therapist because I had a similar life experience. I am so blessed to have this assignment brought to me by the power of the universe. This happens so often in my life. I know who I am, that I am where I need to be, and doing the work I am supposed to be doing.

PRACTICE #1: BE HONEST WITH YOURSELF AND FACE YOUR TRUTH

ANALYSIS

The first step upon learning an ugly truth or experiencing a deep betrayal is to let the pain flow. Really let yourself feel it first, and then shift the grief and anger into something positive. We're not wallowing in our sorrow, people! This way, you're not suppressing the feelings and trapping them in your body but rather processing them and releasing them so you can free up space for more goodness.

Letting it flow is a key point for healing: You *will* survive hearing the truth, and you *will* be freed from carrying the weight of the deception. By finding out the truth, you can heal yourself by realizing that "the big lie" is no longer *your* story. By allowing your mind to have control over your emotional pain, you can even find empathy for those deceivers in your life.

This is a process, and there is no hurry—healing will come with time. Remember, everyone does the best they can in each moment with the tools they have. We all make mistakes and it's now your job is to step forward into finding your voice and your power as an individuated person who isn't hiding in the shadow of lies.

PERSONAL ASSESSMENT

Answer the following questions in your journal:

1. Has anything ever shocked you in your life where you feel like the rug was pulled out beneath you?

2. List or name 3 positive results of learning some of the ugly truths.

3. Now that you know the truth, you can be free and you can trust that you're free. Journal about how you are practicing surrender and trust as a new way to be.

4. Say this Affirmation daily: I can handle any information, as long as it's the truth. I belong to me. *If it's to be, it's up to me.*

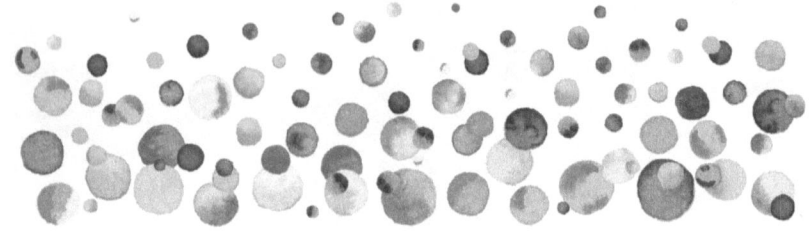

I forgive others with ease and grace.

PRACTICE #2

Let Go and Forgive

"Forgiveness is not always easy. At times, it feels more painful than the wound we suffered, to forgive the one that inflicted it. And yet, there is no peace without forgiveness."

—MARIANNE WILLIAMSON

FORGIVING THE UNFORGIVABLE

One rule I learned long ago still helps me every day: *nobody knows what it's like to be you, the inside you, the you locked-away—the true-you.* If you have a physical disability, psychological disability, or any other limitation, often no one takes the time to get to know you at all. If someone is cruel, or hurts your feelings, remember this: "You" are really the inside person, and the individual who is picking on you has no clue what a fabulous creature you *really are*. Forgive, forget, move on. Our time is precious. Don't waste yours in a stew of anger.

My patients sometimes refer to "unforgivable" actions—abuse, traumas and the perpetrators who have gone beyond the limits of forgiveness. I don't tell them right away that *nothing is unforgivable*...I listen to their stories, and I feel their pain with them...I know pain, so relating is easy. New patients have to tell their story before healing can start—and once their trash is empty, the work of *forgiveness* begins.

We need to first deconstruct our stories, and then reconstruct them in the way we want our lives to go.

For me, growing up was pure hell. There is really no other way to put it. I was never grounded, never secure, always waiting for the next family crisis.

What is considered unforgivable? My mother's diabolical meddling, meanness and constant verbal abuse? Or my father's angry tirades and vicious beatings? I certainly couldn't imagine forgiving them at the time. Like I said, life was pure hell.

RUN AWAY

When I was 13 years old, I remember making a big decision: I was not going to take the abuse anymore. Between my father beating up the family every chance he had, and my mother's verbal abuse, I was done. I had hit a wall. I couldn't take it anymore.

I was ready to leave and start a new life, but unfortunately, I was only 13 and knew almost nothing about how things worked, so my big plan was to run away and become a nun. I could try that for awhile, and if it didn't work out, I would turn to prostitution! Somehow, it made sense at the time, and I was certain I would not be missed by anyone...in fact, my family would rejoice at my disappearance!

My plan never came to fruition, and that same year, my mother gave birth to my miracle brother Gennaro. When I saw him, I knew he needed me. Our family was crazy, so I decided to stay and save him from all the hell. I knew that if I was there, I could protect him. After all, they would not go after him if they had me to kick around! I was used to it, and I decided it was too late for my other brother and I, but if I could save Gennaro, it would all be worth it. So I stayed. The birth of baby Gennaro saved my life. I do not know where I would have ended up had he not come along. I would probably be dead. His presence brought purpose and meaning to my life.

ANALYSIS

Writing this book has reopened some old wounds for me, so the act of forgiving my family is not easy and isn't just a one-time thing—it's on-going. Memories bring back moments that feel unforgivable. How could any father beat his children so badly every year right when Christmas or Easter came around? Especially at a time when as kids, everything around us promised happiness? It's cruel at any point, but to have your holidays consistently become trials of abuse really feels unforgivable. However, healing only comes when you have truly forgiven those who have wronged you, and when you've freed yourself of all the guilt and shame that you've picked up from your life experiences.

Your first step is to get your story out. Write it down free form and let it flow without editing it. No one needs to read this but you. (And once you're done, I want you to actually burn it—in a safe space like a fireplace or outside in a grill or fire-pit.) The longer you stay in your story, the longer you will suffer. It's time to create a new story that reflects a different view of life and the person you are on the inside. Take it one step at a time and know that anything that comes up is fair game for forgiveness.

PRACTICE 2: LET GO AND FORGIVE

It may also be a good idea for you to get some extra healing support during this forgiveness phase. Remember, the most important person to forgive is YOURSELF for any shame and guilt that you have carried as a way of developing healthy coping mechanisms. You are not alone! This is an exercise in cultivating compassion for yourself and/or the abuser.

PERSONAL ASSESSMENT

Answer the following questions in your journal:

1. What is the most unforgivable thing that has ever happened in your life?

2. What effect has this had on your life?

3. Imagine the abuser as simply a wounded child in an adult's body who is repeating their own story of abuse at the hands of someone else...can you feel empathy for their own pain that may have caused their terrible behavior?

4. Once you have written your old story of trauma, burn it in a fire pit or fireplace.

5. Then write down your most loving words of forgiveness towards your abusers. Keep this in a safe place to read again whenever you get triggered or need to release anger or shame.

6. Feel the freedom from releasing the pain and embracing love and forgiveness for anyone who has ever hurt you. Journal about your experience.

BABY GIULIA AND HER PARENTS

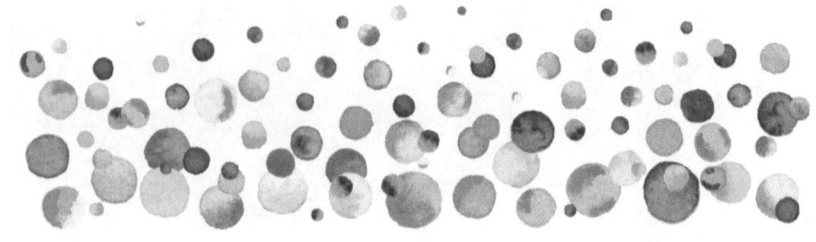

I listen to the wisdom of my body.

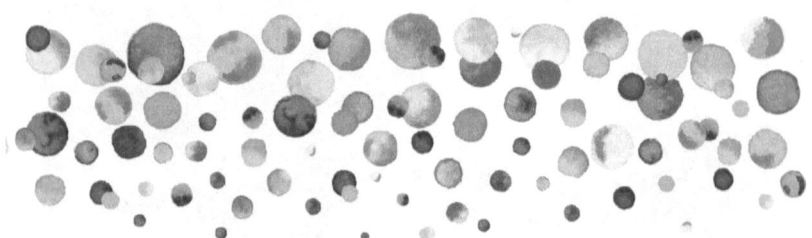

PRACTICE #3

Trust Your Body Wisdom

BAT SONAR

Whenever I said anything important, my family immediately went into attack mode. I usually blurted out my big news with my nerves on fire, knowing full well what was to come from my "loving and supportive" family. For instance, when I wanted to go to college, I walked into the living room and announced my plan. Like clockwork, my mother reminded me I would never be able to succeed, scolded me because I couldn't see well enough to go to school (thanks for reminding me, Mom!), and of course her favorite wish in the whole world—that I had never been born.

My Dad was quiet, watching my mother carry on—and he didn't bring it up until the week before my first semester. Getting ready was fun, and I was *excited!* This was my big break! I'm surprised, looking back, that I didn't realize it was too good to be true.

The week before I was going to go to college my father told me he was not going to pay for my tuition because I was a girl.

What?! Why?!

He explained in his very matter-of-fact, *here is my word and you-will-obey* voice that he was *not* going to invest in a *girl*. I was so mad! I asked him why he let it go so far before telling me—and he said he thought for sure I was going to back down after my mother (and my family) worked on me. Then he reminded me, once again, that I should have been a man. This just made me crazy! He said—again—that I had guts that women never have. My father *did* respect me—which may sound weird, given the number of times he had beaten and belittled me—but I knew that on a deep level, he actually *admired* my spirit, my tenacity, and my courage.

Here is the truth: When you have a disability, it can feel like you will never get a break, like you can never truly *breathe* with freedom. Not only do you have to navigate the world without a full set of tools, but the bar to prove yourself is set *higher* for us than "normal" people, and we usually get blamed first for any screw-ups. Survival depends on being one step ahead, if possible!

So I decided to go to cosmetology school and pay for it myself.

However, I knew that once I got into cosmetology school, I'd need a ride to get there. (Dad certainly wasn't going to be any help!) My options were few, so I used my "bat sonar" to find the person who could get *me what I needed to survive and go forward.* (Bat Sonar was my way of paying VERY close attention to the situation and what was needed.) I was optimistic! I found someone to drive me to school, and I was off...

I have had many drivers in my life, some good, some bad. One of the toughest experiences I had was with one particular person who drove me during the last several years of getting my undergraduate degree in college.

It became clear during our first ride that this woman was demeaning and cruel. She was the extreme opposite of me — but I still had to get to school, so I just had to deal with it to get my ride. I had exhausted all other options including paying a cab service.

Every day in that car with her, I felt a pain inside. She would talk about politics that I didn't agree with — I could easily nod my head and "uh-huh" through that part of the ride! But it got tougher to deal with when she would talk about how she hated her own daughter because she was fat and a "pain in the ass". She talked about her daughter the way my mother would talk about me.

My inner-voice never stopped on these rides. "I am not good enough, I'm never going to be loved by my mother, I am a piece of shit!" echoed through my mind while I waited for the next ugly diatribe from my driver.

Some days she talked about her sex life, telling me things that I *never* wanted to hear—from anyone! Every day of my life, panic and fear were my default emotions, and the rides to school almost broke me. I always shook inside, and when I tried to speak, the words never came out right. I would bite my nails, and just try to stay invisible. My mind never stopped, I was always hiding inside, waiting for the next horror to unfold...

Only when I lay in bed at night could I actually exhale. Whew...I survived another day.

Looking back, I can't *imagine* how I survived it all. I felt I had no other choice if I wanted to finish school. I know there have been times in my life when the world would have said I was stubborn, but looking back, there was a guiding voice in me that I could never turn off.

PRACTICE #3: TRUST YOUR BODY WISDOM

You know that old saying, "Blind as a bat," right? Well, that was me! Yet, even though I am considered legally blind, I have been blessed with more sight then anyone could ever imagine. I can see things that people will never see. I see things that the human eye cannot. I feel things that most people cannot. I am thankful for it all. But it was *blind faith* that got me to where I found my true self, and now I am following my calling every day, sharing my story, and guiding others towards their own freedom.

But back then, it was my parents who were kind enough to remind me that I couldn't see—all day, every day. And also, I was stupid, lazy, fat, ugly, unwanted, and unloved. And that was before breakfast! (By the way, I'm laughing right now, and I hope you are, too! If my story was a TV sitcom, we would all be hysterical, knowing that as soon as I put my superhero costume on, I will *smash* the bad guys! It's my show, and I always win!)

So how could a short, squeaky-voiced blind-as-a-bat girl survive all of this and end up sitting on this side of the therapy desk?

Sonar. Yup, bats again. The irony of being *blind as a bat* is that by using their built-in radar, bats can *see* better than if they had eyes! Bat sonar lets the spooky little beasts fly at night like crazed jets on a secret bug-eating mission! Human sonar is different, though. I've never tried flying at night, but I use my radar all the time by sensing into a person's energy, and then trusting my intuition and the messages my body is telling me.

Here's the truth and the hard facts: To survive my life, I needed help—and lots of it. I had developed self-reliance, and I knew I would get past whatever stood in my way, yet, I needed help to get where I needed to be! So I used my sonar power to connect with people who would offer a hand. I focused on *knowing what they needed from me* so I could get what *I needed from them*. Here's an example:

I was so scared when my mom would say, "You should have died—we both should have died!" I never knew what to do, so I learned what she wanted to hear and I'd tell her, "You're a good mom". Then she'd be off my back. I would apologize for being alive. Of course, if my dad heard me do that, he'd get furious and say, "Be brave and courageous!" When they were together, I didn't speak because Dad would say, "Shut your mouth". I never knew what I needed to do for the day to survive. I felt NO freedom. I was just an actor in their crazy drama. So, I used my sonar to understand what I needed to do to get the ride. I adapted, like a chameleon to the situation. I *had* to do it. *Determination* was my power, and whatever obstacles I met in my path were fuel for my journey.

ANALYSIS

Trust your body wisdom—it never lies.

We have all heard the statement "the end justifies the means" many times, but it has special meaning to anyone struggling to get help, get noticed, and *survive* with a disability or a challenge. Standing up for yourself doesn't mean alienating those who can help you—even if they are "blind" to the "real" you beneath the physical disability they see. There were many times I had to bite my tongue—hard!—to hold in my voice...yet, I knew my survival depended on having to be with people I may not like or be comfortable around, and making the choice to get my needs met.

When something stands in the way of your goal, you need to fight! Be your own biggest advocate! And use your bat sonar to understand others, how you can align with and help them, and how they can help you move forward.

PERSONAL ASSESSMENT

Answer the following questions in your journal:

1. How do you identify a gut feeling and trust that it's true for you?

2. Was there ever a time that you trusted your body wisdom and it was right? Did it surprise you?

3. How can you discern the right choice based on your intuition and not on all the information that you've been fed?

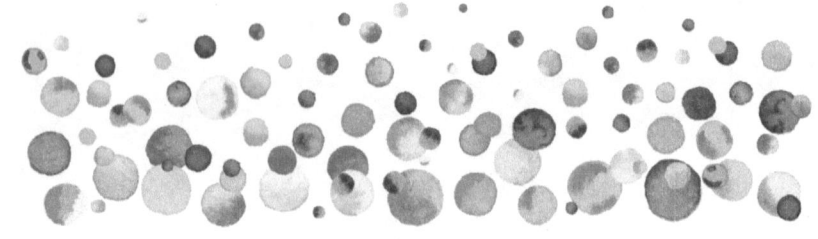

*I love myself and trust that
I have all the answers inside.*

PRACTICE #4

Build Your Self-Confidence

NEVER QUITE GOOD ENOUGH...

One day while at my graduate school internship, my supervisor announced that I had to disclose my condition of Macular Degeneration to all my therapy clients at the start at each session. I took issue with this, because not only was this a violation of the therapeutic process but it also started out each session with the focus on me and not on the client. The client is coming in with *their* problems, they certainly do not need to hear about mine!

Sigh. How did I get here again? How can this be? Will this ever not *be the case for me?*

I had worked hard to be accepted into the program and begin my life journey as a therapist. I was so looking forward to being in an institution that understood about people's differences, equality, and took a stand to support each person's gifts. I desired a community where I was not going to be treated differently and feel like a freak of nature, a pariah, or just someone that they needed to tolerate until they could prove that my vision truly made it impossible for me to perform...and then they could get rid of me.

Not again! How did I end up in this same position? I could not believe it. It must've been a joke, or maybe I was dreaming and was going to wake up...But it was real. This was so painful, my head felt like it was going to explode and my heart hurt. It felt so cruel and disappointing.

At first, I became so angry that I began to shake as the supervisor was speaking to me. I stopped breathing, as I had done so many times before, but then I took a deep breath and said, "NO. I am not going to do that." I could not believe the words had come out of my mouth. I finally stood up and said it! It was scary and so freeing at the same time. "First of all, that goes against the therapeutic process and second of all, it's against the ADA law." I said. As her chin dropped to the floor and her eyes got as big as the full moon, she responded, "We will see about that."

PRACTICE #4: BUILD YOUR SELF-CONFIDENCE

And so it began, the continual journey of having to prove myself over and over again. I was being watched carefully and was not trusted to do the job well because I had a visual limitation. I knew the script. I could write the story before it even unfolded before my eyes.

This was another truth I needed to finally face: that my life was always going to be like this unless *I* could change my attitude and how I felt. I was ready. The view was different, but the path was the same—*different play, same game*. I wasn't worried, just sad. I wasn't afraid, just tired. I knew it was the establishment's fear and not mine. Once they got to know me—the real me, not the "blind girl"—it would be good enough for them to "let me" be there. The sad part was the realization that no matter what I did, it was not never going to be good enough, *ever*. I did not want to have to do this for the rest of my life! There was no end to the process for Giulia the blind girl. My poor vision was all that people could see, not my humanity.

It was time for me to create my own feeling of worthiness, instead of waiting for it to come from the outside—and just be me...take it or leave it!

I realized for the first time that this was my legacy in life and there was no escaping it, and that day, a part of my heart broke. *Some people get it, but most people just hear my words, and don't see the* person *behind the words.*

They were so stuck in limitation and fear of the situation that the real me was invisible.

Even though my heart was broken that day, it did not bury me! I knew in the deepest part of my soul that I had a greater purpose. I knew life was going to continue to be painful, but I was ready because I knew that I needed to face myself and my purpose—no matter what came my way.

And so I kept going.

Back to the supervisor.

After an extensive conversation, not surprisingly, she reported me to the school and to the agency as being defiant and resistant to authority. This issue became the main focus for several months, but in the meantime, I performed all that was required of me and continued to prove myself over and over again. Whatever I did must have been good enough, because by the end of my internship, I was offered a full-time position and worked for the agency for many years after. How about that? The "blind girl" was competent after all!

ANALYSIS

For me, one of the hardest parts of living with a disability has been finding my self-confidence when I know that people are looking at me like I'm from another planet! People with disabilities have to deal with the stigma of our impairments, knowing that for most people, we're not seen, and we don't matter.

Here's the part that you need to fully understand: None of this really matters, because we're not defined by the people outside of us. No one knows who we *really* are so how can *anyone* make a judgment?

You must find the love in your heart for yourself.

As long as you know deep down that you're special and that you have all that you need inside of you to succeed, your self-confidence will keep bouncing back no matter how many times you fall down. It takes time and patience, and it comes after the accomplishment is complete. The more you accomplish, the more you will prove to yourself that you are worthy and can do it. Show yourself what you can do and then build on it. Tap into your inherent worthiness and inner authority...and celebrate you!

PERSONAL ASSESSMENT

Answer the following questions in your journal:

1. Do you constantly feel the judgment of others? Do you judge yourself? If so, how does it make you feel?

2. Describe 5 qualities about yourself that you love.

3. What are your strengths?

4. Say the following affirmation morning and evening for the next 7 days: "I love myself and trust that I have all the answers inside." Journal your insights.

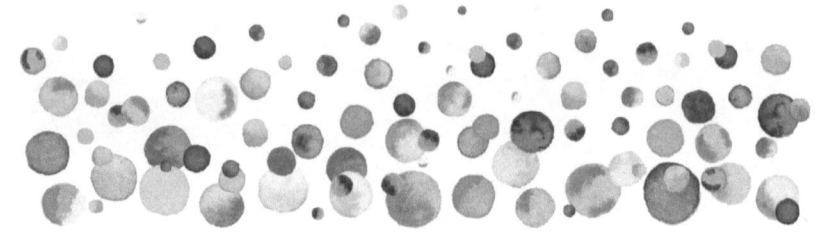

My power is always in the present moment.

PRACTICE #5

Stand Up for Yourself, Speak Your Truth, and Find Your Power

No one can create your life but you. No one can show your potential but you. This means you have to say NO sometimes, or set a boundary with a family member, child, friend, stranger, sibling, or partner. You have to stand tall for your truth and be willing to act accordingly. Be YOU. Know YOU. What are your mind, body, and spirit saying?

Stand up for yourself! Find your power!

We have all heard it. It sounds easy, but what if you can't see and need help to navigate the big world out there? And, just as an example — on top of a physical disability, imagine having a mother who never said a positive word, and a father who waited for me to take 1-step forward just so he could drag me back 2 or 3 steps?

Honestly, it took a long time for me to feel anything close to power.

I was usually petrified, anxious, frozen—afraid to breathe. These sensations never seemed to leave me but still I had to take action despite my fear and anxiety. I began to use my fear as my guide. The more I was afraid the more I fought for what I felt was right—so I pushed forward but in doing so, also pushed my scared inner child aside, instead of embracing her. I was too busy trying to survive. At that time, I had no other choice. I stood up for myself when I could, but my reactions were more "fight or flight" than anything else.

I had no clue that my "truth" was anything more than long days filled with confusion and hurt, and fretful nights spent sleeplessly dreading the dawn. I went to bed in fear and I woke up in fear. Fear was my norm, my baseline. Down deep I knew there was more for me in this life. I somehow knew that I had to go through this for the greater good, and that everything was a lesson.

Here is what I learned: On the other side of that pain is the true gift, and once you begin to stand up for yourself and speak your truth, you'll feel more and more empowered, people around you will respond to you differently, and you'll feel others holding a new level of respect for your presence. If you can't hold that power, no one else will, so the time is ripe to embrace the pain as your teacher. Don't ignore the reality of what you're experiencing! The pain will be there, and you will feel it but do not let it stop you. Eventually, after a few times of speaking up, the pain will not be so loud and you will feel yourself getting braver and braver. The courage and the fear will sing together as you need to do what you need to do. Accept that as strange as this sounds, the fear is there for a reason. You don't need to like it, but you do need to figure out what it is trying to tell you. Fear, just like joy and happiness, plays an important part in our ability to survive. Do not let it rule you, just listen to the message it is trying to give you. Now you can let your greater purpose unfold and stick with it through the painful parts.

MOM BREAKS IN

One day, I was standing outside of my mother's house arguing with her. This was not an unusual event. She had been attempting to break into my home again but this time the door was locked. Then she tried to climb through a window but was unable to fit through.

Yep, that's my mom. She wanted me to leave my door unlocked at all times and when it wasn't, she would become *incensed*. You see, my mother's house was behind mine, so she thought she owned the place—meaning *my home*.

She was saying the usual things to me: *I wish you were dead; I wish you had never been born, you are a loser, you destroy everyone and everything you come in contact with*...I was used to it. I ignored those things because I believed that someday she would change her mind. I truly believed I could somehow win her over, win over her heart, her love. But then she said something I had never heard her say before.

She began to compare me to my female cousins. She named them all by name and smiled at me as she was saying what a loser I was compared to them. Then she said she wished that *they* were her daughters instead of me. She said she was so mad for getting stuck with the blind, dumb one. At that moment I felt a rush across my heart and then my body began to shake uncontrollably. I remember saying to myself, "Wow, she really means that". I began to cry, and she curled her lips and kept smiling.

It was at that moment that she left my heart.

I looked at her and said, "I will never let you hurt me again. You just left my heart." That was the day I freed myself from her cruelty—and everything changed because I finally was able to let go of the need for my mother's approval. I didn't need to please her any longer. I only needed to focus on myself and what was best for me. It was freeing—and also crippling—because I no longer needed my mother's approval to feel good or validated for being alive. The pain was still there but so was the grief, loss, and mourning for the mother I could never have. But I was in full acceptance of my life at last—and it was a good thing.

FINDING YOUR POWER

Power is something we all need to come to grips with and it starts when we are children. If you are lucky, you have a healthy body and supportive parents who will guide you to find your *zing* and fill your skin with confidence. If you were *me,* almost everyone worked their hardest to *stomp* my power before I had a chance to figure anything out! Many parents take out their own deep feelings of inadequacy on their children, and mine made undermining me a full-time pursuit—I was *everyone's sacrificial lamb!* And unfortunately, my father seemed to take particular pleasure in humiliating me in public.

He would take me out, fully knowing that I couldn't see for beans. Inevitably, someone would ask me something, or I'd run into a chair, and rather than supporting me and explaining that I had a vision problem, my father would look at me, see how embarrassed I was, and then, loud enough for all to hear, would say, *"She's stupid."* I felt utterly powerless. There was absolutely nothing I could do to defend who I really was and what was *really* going on.

School was a horror story—so much so that some nights I would pray to not wake up in the morning. I was about 20 pounds overweight and was not allowed to dress like the other kids. I couldn't wear jeans and most of my clothes were either too small or too big for me. I was also always two years older than the other kids in my class because I was born in Italy and there was a language barrier. The powers that be thought it would help me and all the other Italian students learn the language better. I never understood the logic of that...but with my inability to see well enough to read the board, I was trapped.

I would enter each classroom and pretend I was invisible. I thought that if I pretended to be invisible, I would not get called upon to answer a question. Unfortunately that did not work. I was laughed at each time I said I could not read aloud because I could not see to read the text. The teachers would ask me when I was going to stop saying that and try another excuse. Each and every time, I never got a break—they didn't believe me! But I kept on going and kept on doing the best I could. I had no other choice! I was finding my power, and learning how to claim it.

PRACTICE #5: STAND UP FOR YOURSELF

At one point, I went from being an excellent reader, to not being able to hardly see at all. I remember the word "canoe" in 3rd grade. My teacher pointed to the screen and asked, "Who can figure out how to read this word?"

If I sounded it out right, I could read it.

Canoe.

But by the next month, I couldn't see the word at all. I couldn't tell my teacher why. I hid my head in my book, and of course I got scolded. But I wasn't allowed to tell her I couldn't see! In my powerlessness, I always followed the rules and did what I was told.

Finally at age 10, even though my mother said no, I made the appointment to get my eyes checked. You see, that was a time when many people were immigrating to America from Italy and the adults did not speak English. Therefore, the children were their parents' interpreters. So when I called to set up the appointment and told them that my mother and father did not speak English, they granted me the appointment. I was so excited! I hoped the doctor could give me glasses and it would fix everything. I finally was able to convince my mother to come with me, so she and my brother and I walked to the appointment. My mom was not able to speak the language, so I explained to the receptionist that I was her interpreter.

After he examined me, the doctor told my mother that I needed to go to a specialist in Boston. Turns out my problems were bigger than glasses. My mother response was, "Thank god you can't wear glasses, at least you won't look like a cripple." I could not believe what I was hearing! Instead of being concerned about my condition, she was concerned about how I would look with glasses. As an 11-year-old with no power, I was shocked and afraid—I had no idea what to do next, and was fearful of going totally blind. What was I going to do?

The fear and negative words haunted me while I struggled to sleep at night. It was a crazy maze I learned to navigate; mom and dad knew that *their* power came from keeping me from finding out the truth about my eyesight, and it wasn't until I uncovered the secrets lying in the middle of the maze that *my* power took form inside me.

I was not taken to Boston Eye and Ear Hospital as the doctor had recommended. So with poor vision and no end in sight, I had to learn to navigate the world on my own.

PRACTICE #5: STAND UP FOR YOURSELF

ANALYSIS

When you're feeling uncomfortable, being labeled and judged, start showing what you know. Stick them with facts. If anyone asks for an opinion, stand up! Take the risk to start talking.

Mindfulness practice is essential—before you go anywhere, make sure you are centered, aware, and have rehearsed your role. Be on your game. Your job is to know your stuff. Prepare. Shift from being a victim to being your own best advocate—this is your responsibility! You must be determined and have a plan to succeed at all times.

Step into your warrior self, your superhero! Tap into your anger to find motivation, but don't let that consume you. Your internal fire needs to be lit, and it will fuel your journey. The words you use can be evocative of your power.

Love yourself enough to become your own advocate, without needing external validation. When you are feeling the most anxious is when you have to speak up the most, so find a way to speak up and break the cycle. Be true to yourself and to your disability because it's the interface with your world. Find different ways to show your power when necessary—you've got to be tough and do what it takes to get what you need!

You have psychological strength which means you can conquer anything, in spite of what the world brings. Yes, you may have been labeled, and your true image may have been stifled. You've been believing you can't do ANYTHING—but now it's time to blow that belief away and let your warrior emerge!

People with disabilities are usually very protected by parents. Some flourish, some stay cocooned. Whatever your challenge, you are strong and you don't need coddling to make it! What you *do* need is courage and strength. Remember, life is 99% effort, 1% brain power.

PRACTICE #5: STAND UP FOR YOURSELF

PERSONAL ASSESSMENT

Answer the following questions in your journal:

1. How do you express your truth to others?

2. How do you handle obstacles?

3. How do you protect yourself from other people's judgment and from your own self judgment?

4. How do you create boundaries with other people? How do you protect your energy?

5. Are you afraid of groups? How do you find your power when in a group situation?

6. How can you step up and get out of your shell?

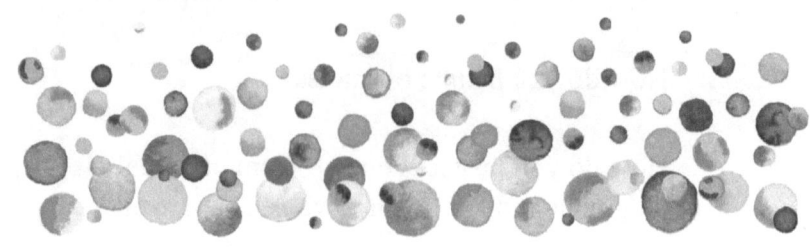

I live in harmony and balance with everyone I know.

PRACTICE #6

Create Healthy Relationships

As you can surely understand by now, I had no idea how to be in a healthy relationship. There were certainly no examples in my family that I could learn from, and when I got married, well, let's just say I had a lot to learn. Unfortunately, my parents never missed a chance to undo any progress I made. I remember one ugly incident in particular that ironically ended up helping my marriage...

It was a hot summer day, the kind of heat that made your skin itchy—and your mood prickly. My husband and I had gotten into a big fight, who knows about what, and my feisty Italian blood was boiling! I may be petite, but my voice is giant! When you let your emotions takeover, you don't care who might be listening, and of course the windows were open, so my parents were able to hear us...The whole neighborhood could hear everything, too! It was certainly not one of my proudest moments.

As we were yelling like complete idiots, there was a knock on the door—then we heard the door open. Oh boy...it was my father. He looked at me with his dark eyes, and then he turned to my husband and said, "Giulia needs a beating. You can't do it because you will go to jail, so I will do it for you." My husband was shocked. After a brief silence, he said, "No! Pa, I do not want to hit her, and neither should you! We are okay—I never want anyone to hit Giulia." My husband then turned to me and apologized. I began to cry and tremble. All of the horror of growing up under the thumb of my father came flooding through me as my he gave me that menacing look. He spoke Italian so Dan wouldn't understand. "I will kill you rather than having you embarrass me by you getting a divorce. You better behave! Who the hell else is going to want YOU?" I did not answer. My husband asked me what he said, and I was unable to answer him. My father wasn't done—he turned to my husband and repeated it in English as best he could. He then sat down and did not leave for two and a half hours. There was complete silence the entire time. It was torture! The only thing that kept me from completely falling apart was my son. He was a baby and I was holding him the entire time in my arms. I still remember the sound of his little heart beating. Finally, Dan asked him to leave. He assured him that he was not going to divorce me, and that he would not allow anyone to hit me, so it would be best to leave.

PRACTICE #6: CREATE HEALTHY RELATIONSHIPS

That was a turning point for my relationship with my husband. Finally, he witnessed firsthand what my life had been like growing up, and to this day he is still in horror, but he understands.

It took me about a week to even start to recover. Post-traumatic stress syndrome is NOT only for soldiers! I was transported back to my darkest days and once again reminded of the lack of validity from my father and mother, and the heartless ways I was treated. Usually it was my mother who tore me down, but this time it was him—my Dad—the one I thought actually loved me.

I was way, way down in my dark hole of self-hatred.

Two weeks later he called me and asked me to come and see him. I didn't want to, but I went anyway. He didn't apologize. Not him...he told me to forget the incident, and to move on. He said he cared about me as much as he could, and that I needed to be a good, loyal daughter. Everything in my family was all about *secrets*...so as usual, he told me to never speak to anyone about what happened.

When I asked him if he would do it again, he said YES.

In my own crazy way, I excused his behavior—again! I blamed it on his culture, his upbringing, and everything else. My parents had taken my power away long ago, and in my weakened state of mind, I gave up. I was certain that I needed to be a great daughter and listen to my father—no matter what.

That is how badly I wished to feel loved.

Today, I forgive him for that. I forgive it all. Really, forgiveness is a gift you can give *yourself*. What happened, happened. I know both of my parents did the best that they could do with what they had. In one way, I wish he could see me now...but then again, I am certain his opinion of me would not change. I am at peace with my life. I am grateful, because I know I was really a good daughter, and I have no regrets.

RENEWAL

After that, my husband Dan and I grew closer. He saw me more clearly, and his empathy made me feel safe. We agreed that our relationship needed to be nurtured, and that we needed to take care of each other's needs. I was ready to go back to school—and together, we decided that Dan would go to school, too, so we could stay on the same path.

Growth in a relationship is critical! I was so hungry to learn, and I knew it was important for Dan to grow, too, to

PRACTICE #6: CREATE HEALTHY RELATIONSHIPS

keep the balance between us. So many doors that I never imagined began to open for me! I am proud to point out that I am my family's first educated female in my generation. I knew it was the beginning of my big break! I was going to break the chains of my family culture, and break the cycle. I really didn't know how to deal with the outside world, but I knew the only way to start something scary and new was to step forward, and start being the real me. It sounds *so easy, right?* I knew I had to change, but how? How do you find out who you are when you've been so stifled? Somehow I found my way.

There was a real "me" in there somewhere...I wanted to keep some of the parts of myself that I liked, *and* fill up those empty spaces where I had released trauma and pain with new choices and a whole new life. I had to give up the old to embrace the new. I couldn't make everything from scratch anymore, but hey! I'm Italian! We bake bread and we make things rise! So I found my balance and stepped forward. It was the end of my old life—and of the beginning of everything new.

My husband only went to school for a few months. He got a job as a cop, and I stayed in school and became a therapist. Even though we took different career paths, the fact that we started in school together was proof of our loyalty to each other, and that we were committed to grow—together. Even healthy relationships need work, and we stuck it out.

One of my best and most meaningful relationships was not with a family member. Some of the best relationships fall outside of family and marriage, since the old stories and baggage don't stand in the way of true understanding. Stewart was my professor, teacher and friend. I'd never had a "real" friendship with an adult, and the vitality of honest communication was so refreshing!

Stewart was charged with the task of getting large-print for my exams, and taping my voice for extended papers. Through this process, he came to *see me*...ME! It was amazing! For the first time, I felt like I was appreciated for my gifts—instead of being judged for my faults. As he came to see me clearly, he reached out more, inviting me to come to his open office hours. He asked me questions about why my writing and my life didn't seem to match up.

"Giulia, you are brilliant to a flaw! You know so much, and your papers are wonderful. But...something is off kilter. When we talk, your life story doesn't connect with your writing."

He was right, of course, and his confusion made sense. Remember, I'm a petite girl, I'm practically blind, my voice is powerful and kind of squeaky, and I was raised by parents who had absolutely no positive parenting skills and were not skilled to parent anyone—let alone a visually-impaired kid like me. It didn't make sense even to me! Yet, over time, Stewart and I found a language to share, and a style of relationship that could grow and be nurtured. He helped me to trust my gut and stand up for myself. I called him on his actions and kept him honest, and when I needed help, he was there for me.

More than anything else, he taught me about *fear*...I was a scared little girl lost in the big world when we found each other, and he helped me to not be afraid—but to see fear as a guide, not a hindrance. Fear kept me frozen, held me back, and after so much abuse growing up, I held my little girl inside me, tightly protected, trusting no one with my wounded soul.

Stewart was different—I trusted him—and as our friendship grew, I let myself just be me, in an adult friendship, for the first time. I mattered to him, and I helped him to be *softer,* and more empathetic towards those who struggle every day to be heard. I taught him how to make bread by hand, the old Italian way, and shared the good things I had learned growing up. We had fun! We grew and adjusted, like friends should, and my world became much brighter because of Stewart. If I was ever hesitant, I would call him, and he would tell me to "stop getting stuck in the stuff". He told me that life was full of stuff needing to be fixed, so to just stop it and move on. I knew what that meant, and I knew where to go after that each and every time. He really knew me and helped to spark my internal fire that would sometimes dim. Unfortunately his fire no longer shines. He was taken way too soon from this world.

ANALYSIS

The key to creating healthy relationships is negotiation and truth. Be willing to hear and understand the other person's position, and why they are taking that position. Remember, don't take ANYTHING personally! This person comes to you with their knowledge, and they can only do the best with what they've got. Don't have any expectations—but be willing have boundaries and to speak up for what you need. Be aware of their feelings. Just like you, they have pain, too. As people, we all suffer. Hold compassion for them and yourself. Get out of your head and focus on being the second part of a healthy dynamic.

Do your part! The secret is to meet them where they are without judgment. This doesn't mean you won't experience unhappiness, but be willing to compromise. It doesn't always feel great, but it's a good way to sustain honest communication and compassion. Remember, you get to choose your world, your relationships, and your chosen family. Surround yourself with positive and supportive people who vibrate like you. If people judge and knock you, let go of guilt for transitioning relationships that aren't working for you. Let go of victim energy. Do you want to be a victim, or survivor, or a victor? *Elevate out of just survivor to victor!* Victory is not yours at the expense of others, rather it's the freeing of your empowered self, leaving the cage and taking flight. The answer is inside of you...so just listen and allow it to surface.

PERSONAL ASSESSMENT

Answer the following questions in your journal:

1. How do you bring your best version of you to your relationships?

2. How are your relationships meaningful?

3. How are your relationships toxic?

4. How are these new changes in you affecting your relationships?

5. How can you strengthen your compassion for the other person?

PRACTICE #6: CREATE HEALTHY RELATIONSHIPS

GIULIA WITH FRIEND AND COLLEAGUE HEATHER MCNEIL

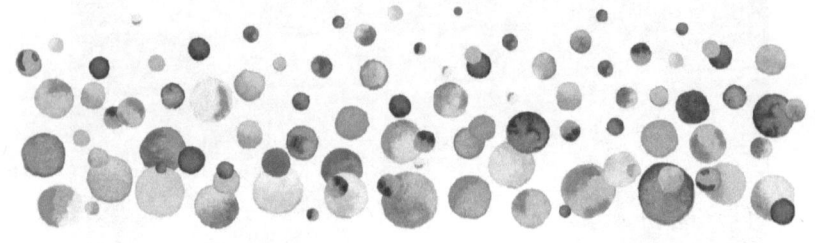

I return to the basics of life: forgiveness, courage, gratitude, love, and humor.

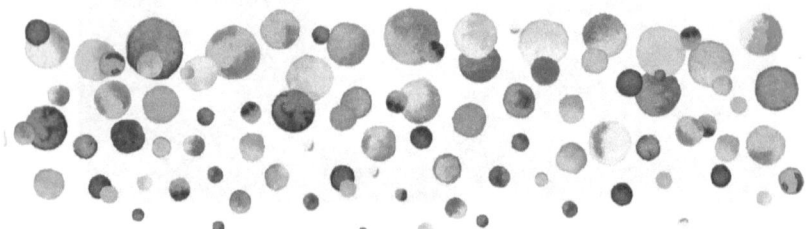

PRACTICE #7

Use Humor and Laugh through Your Pain

DRUG SCREENING

I went to have a drug screening for my job at an agency. As my husband and I approached the front office, the receptionist handed me a stack of papers to fill out. My husband took them and began to read me the questions out loud because the print was too small for me to see.

When we were done with the paperwork, we went to the window to hand it back. When the receptionist began to ask questions, she directed the questions to my husband, so he then turned to me and I answered them. We were familiar with this type of response, in fact usually when people noticed him reading to me, they would no longer even directly speak to me! They would usually assume I was illiterate and stupid!

A few minutes later a nurse came out and asked my husband to ask me to follow. I responded and said okay. We would go to the back room where they had taped bathrooms for the drug screening. She handed me a cup and began to explain the process in a loud and slow manner. I stared at her for a long minute and the assured her that I could hear and understand her so please to speak in her regular voice. After she was done, she asked me where my janitor's job was going to be. "Janitor..." I said, "is that what you think I do for a living? Where did you get that idea from?"

"Well, since you can't read, I figured it out," she said. I laughed so hard. It took me a few minutes to gather myself up. Then I explained to her who I really was and why I was not able to complete my paperwork. Her eyes got really big and she paused for a long moment. She then disclosed that she was recently diagnosed with Macular Degeneration. She reported she knew she would be fired once her employer found out. I felt badly for her. She appeared so lost. I then began to tell her where she could go to obtain resources. I told her to keep in touch with me.

A year later, I heard back from her. She wanted to thank me for all the info I had shared. She reported that she was able to use most of the resources I had given her and was able to keep her job because of the new adaptive equipment that helped her perform her job. I was so glad for her!

ANALYSIS

It's okay to be different. You have the power to change the subject and stay in the moment while finding the humor in the situation. One time, my tutor had such bad breath—but I couldn't tell her because I didn't want to hurt her feelings. I tolerated it the whole time, then I chuckled all the way to the bathroom where I immediately threw up! You don't have to bestow on everybody your truth, just be authentic— and allow yourself to see the humor in the struggle.

When you listen and look for the humor behind the pain, you are cultivating kindness towards yourself and the other person. Turn this into a practice of deep listening and then identifying something positive that can be shared as humor. Once I went for an interview, and when I met the supervisor who was supposed to hire me, he asked, "What can you see?" I responded, "I can see that you are bald!" This broke the ice tremendously. It's okay to use some sarcasm but be strategic in what you say because there is a fine line between being funny and hurtful, so stay focused on "kind" humor.

Break any judgment you feel with humor, bringing the focus off of your disability. When I tell people that I am "blind as a bat" they become curious about me rather than expressing pity. People will accept you with humor, so try breaking the judgment flow with a funny shock-factor. Laughing at your self is an act of self-love! (Oh, and by the way, in this book, I can make fun of myself, but you cannot make fun of me!)

PERSONAL ASSESSMENT

Answer the following questions in your journal:

1. How do you use humor to shift a stressful situation?

2. How and when do you give yourself permission to laugh at yourself?

3. How do you embrace your humor?

4. How do you use humor not as a defense but as a way of staying connected?

5. How are you aware of when humor is inappropriate?

6. Is your humor self-deprecating? Write about this...and stop doing it! It's not funny.

7. Who do you give permission to be funny with you?

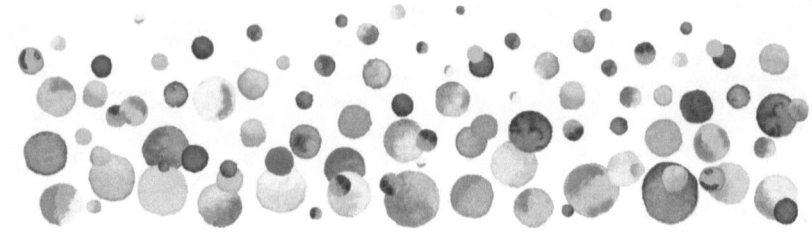

*It is now safe for me to release
all of my childhood traumas
and move into love.*

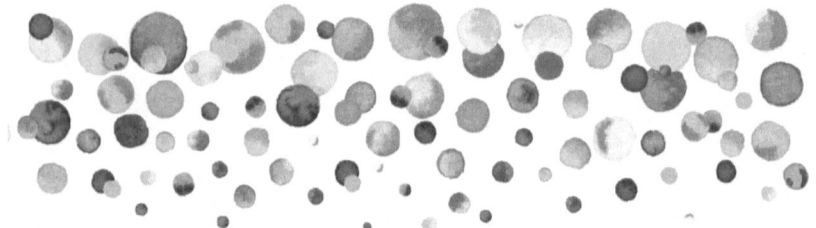

PRACTICE #8

Don't Take Anything Personally

Hey, we don't know what we don't know, right? *Forgiveness* and *surrender* are key to mastering the practice of not taking anything personally. When you can take the high road by not taking anything personally, then you will avoid unnecessary whacks to your self-esteem and be able to sustain your relationships, protect your soul, and your integrity.

You must keep your boundaries and remember that other people's judgments are false. They may never be able to understand your full range of capacities, so you MUST keep your reaction to that under control so you don't get lost in anger. They are literally projecting their own subconscious feelings or fears onto you! You have to be your own driving force. Whatever is true for YOU, that is what you need to trust. Follow your guidance. Be certain that your strength only comes from within. If you're looking outside of yourself, you'll likely be disappointed and won't reach your goals.

If you haven't read *The Four Agreements* by Don Miguel Ruiz, go get it at the library, or find it on Amazon.com. It contains very important truths, expressed simply and beautifully—the most meaningful section for me is the second section, "Don't take anything personally". Think about that for a second...

Don't take anything personally.

Chances are, you take everything personally! We all do it, and it's a big reason most people live in a state of disharmony. If you examine the last couple of times you were angry, or hurting, I'll bet it started with another person's comments or opinion, right? Sadly, most people's default is to cut each other down—when it's really their *own* garbage that they are throwing at you. If you choose to listen, and let your feelings be affected, you are setting yourself up for a tough time.

You alone are responsible for how you feel. No one has the right to mess with your well-being, unless you allow it—so now we are breaking that pattern. This sounds easy, but believe me, it often takes years to develop the self-confidence needed to hold to your own truth when others decide to take you down a peg or two. You may even find yourself *defending* your attackers, wrongly as-

PRACTICE #8: DON'T TAKE ANYTHING PERSONALLY

suming that they have your best interests in mind and are trying to help. Be wary, but also remember that trust takes practice!

When you stop letting others define you or let their words hurt you, freedom becomes a reality—and you can finally feel confidence in YOU and your abilities, without taking two steps back every time your friends and family decide to let you hear *their* version of you, and all the ways you *don't* measure up to their expectations. Remember this and use it daily:

If it's to be, it's up to me!

You are the boss! Whether you are disabled or not, you create your world by finding your own voice—but that is no good to you unless you *use* it. So get to know yourself first, find your power, and take responsibility for the world you create.

At this point in my story, you understand the enormity of my challenge. 99% of the people in my life judged me without batting an eye. I was the "dumb, blind girl"—an easy tag when you don't take the time to find out there might be more hiding behind someone's disability.

Think about if there is someone in your family, or a friend, who has taken the time to know and appreciate the "real you" and offer you the support you need. As

I look back, my family was my biggest problem—and my home was no sanctuary. After fighting for my own identity and purpose all day at school, most of the time I came home to anger, and my parents not getting along.

I was so confused. If my mom and dad hated me, then what was the point of living? My life outside home truly sucked—and when I thought about the next day while tossing in my bed at night, all I could do was imagine how to end my suffering.

I remember literally wanting to die for my mother. I figured if I was dead, it would ease her heart, because I truly *believed* I was a mistake and a freak. I would do it; I'd decided! But then my father would step in, talk to me and convince me otherwise. He pushed me to be better, and then I actually felt good—although it was temporary because I didn't trust him, was so confused, and didn't know my place in this world. My belief systems were completely skewed because of what I had experienced.

Through all of this, I somehow knew that I needed to stay alive for some greater good, and I wanted to believe that my mother really did love me. Plus as cruel as my father could be, there were times when he attempted to guide me. He would tell me he wanted me to be tough and think like a man. He did not want me to let anyone hurt me. He used to tell me I was smart and I needed to make him proud. There was a side to him that he would

PRACTICE #8: DON'T TAKE ANYTHING PERSONALLY

show me at times that was truly caring and endearing. I used to feel so sorry for him—there was something about him that to this day I cannot explain. In my heart, I knew love was available to me, somewhere...

As you might imagine, as a young child I struggled to be loyal to my mother. Her beliefs were built around fear. I tried to understand her reasons for keeping my vision problem a secret, but I also needed to be able to see—and function!

We are all naturally inclined to trust our mothers, aren't we? Like baby birds in the nest, we enter life programmed to depend on our moms—and when that bond is broken, again and again, this essential relationship is fractured.

I wanted to love my mother. I never wanted to hurt her. I spent my life trying to be accepted by her. I always felt her judgment and tried not to embarrass her or the family. Even to this day, I have compassion for her pain and still have the feeling that she really did deserve a different daughter—one that *she* wanted, the little girl of her dreams. Doesn't everyone deserve to have their wants and needs met? I am so sorry she got stuck with me, I truly am. To this day, I still wish that I could have made it better for her growing up. But that was not my purpose or my destiny.

One method of healing a fractured relationship is to write a letter to the person who you are struggling with. This IS NOT a letter to be sent to them or shared with them! The only person who should see this is YOU—and your therapist, if you desire. I decided to write my mother and father the letters I held in my heart, knowing that even if I did decide to actually send them, my parents would never truly understand my feelings or give me what I "wanted" from them. Letting my feelings out on paper—and then burning them—was very healing. I highly recommend you do the same in order to find forgiveness in your heart for the people who hurt you. See if you can identify the gift in the mess that you experienced with that person—gratitude will hasten the healing process dramatically!

Dear Mom,

I want you to know some things that I have had in my heart since I was a little girl...I would like to start off by thanking you for doing the best you could. You made sure that I always had clean clothes and plenty of food to eat, and as you and I both know, I can eat! I know you tried to make me the best you thought I could be. I want to thank you for being honest with your thoughts, even though they were hurtful at the time. At least I always knew what was on your mind! I want to

PRACTICE #8: DON'T TAKE ANYTHING PERSONALLY

tell you that I was always on a quest to please you. I tried my best to be the good little girl that you desired. I am sorry that I wasn't what you hoped for. As a mother myself, I can understand how important having a "perfect little baby" was to you. I wish in my heart and soul that you had gotten that. I now know how difficult it must've been for you to hear that your little girl was never going to see well. Awful words to hear! I am certain I would have not known what to do or what to feel if it was me.

I know the terrible things you said to me like, "I wish you were never born" and " You are an embarrassment" were your way of coping with all that you had to do for me and the sacrifices you had to make. I also believe that each time you pointed out my faults it was because you really wanted to make me the best I could be, even though it did not feel like that at the time. I can't imagine the fear you faced when we walked to my eye appointment. I know you were afraid that I would have to wear glasses and that you would be judged for it.

Mom, I am not you, but I know you did the best you could. I was angry with you many times in my life—it was hard to be your daughter. I am sorry that our relationship was not a close one. More than anything, I want you to know that I forgive you for all the negative things we experienced together in our mother-daughter relationship. I forgive all of it, and I hope you can forgive me for all that I was not able to be for you.

I love you Mom.

When my dad passed away, I lost my grounding. Even though he was abusive and often cruel, I knew he loved me in his own way, and respected my strength—even as he had smacked me and tried to break me. I needed to forgive him, too...

Dear Papa,

I want to write to you to let you know how I feel about you .

Even though you have passed on to the other side, I know in my heart that you are with me, and able to receive what I am about to write.

I want you to know that I learned a lot from you. You taught me how to be strong and to never give up. You wanted me to be "strong like a man" and even though your words sound sexist today, I understand what you meant and that was the only way you could express it. Please know that I have developed strength that few men can equal! Without you pushing me, I am not sure if I would have

PRACTICE #8: DON'T TAKE ANYTHING PERSONALLY

developed the courage and strength that it takes to make it in this world!

You were a wise man in your own right, and I appreciate all that you shared with me and taught me.

There were times that I hated you and everything you did to our family. As awful as that was, I know you felt you were doing the right thing. I know you truly believed it. Your intentions may have seemed good in your mind—but your approach was not.

I want you to know that I forgive you, Dad, for all the bad times. I miss you and love you.

As hard as it was to put these words on paper, I am so glad I did, and am extremely grateful for my close friends, my husband Dan, and my kids for supporting me and loving me through all of it.

PERSONAL ASSESSMENT

Answer the following questions in your journal:

1. Who in your life has taken the time to know and appreciate the "real you" and offer you the support you need? Make a list of those who have supported you and also those who you need to forgive for NOT supporting or "getting" you.

2. When was the last time someone offended you with their words or projections? What did they say that stung? Allow yourself to love that part of you (most likely your inner child) that was hurt.

3. How can you diffuse a situation where you are being judged or attacked?

PRACTICE #8: DON'T TAKE ANYTHING PERSONALLY

4. Write a letter to your mother and father, finding gratitude for what they DID do for you, even if it's simply that they brought you life! Vent your anger, and then allow yourself to feel forgiveness. (DO NOT give these letters to your parents. Instead, offer them to the greater good by burning them and releasing them as a ritual.)

5. Take radical responsibility for your feelings by feeling them first, and then releasing them. How can you become more aware of what you are feeling?

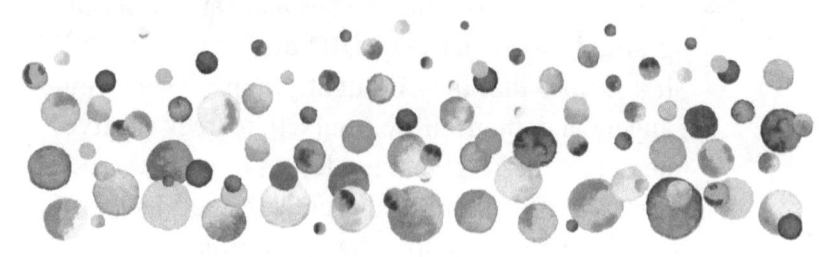

All is well within my world.

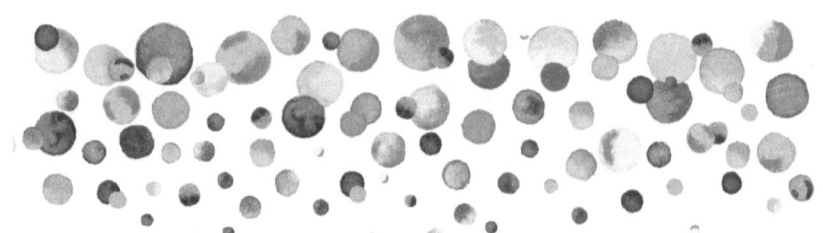

Afterword

A friend of mine once said, "If, within the course of a lifetime, you have as many friends as you have fingers on one hand, consider yourself blessed."

Well, today I consider myself blessed.

One time I had to appear in court for a specific case I was involved in. I had to go before the judge several times. This judge took the time to speak with me about going back to school and doing something "better" with my life. I shared my fears with him and disclosed the limitations I had with my vision. He really cared! And he gave me the resources I needed. He discussed the adaptive equipment that was available, and the new ADA laws that would protect me through the process.

I am so thankful to this man. Without him, I likely would not be where I am today. I wish I could talk to him face to face and tell him that there are great laws in disability, but there is very little heart behind those laws. He took a chance on me, and I feel such gratitude for him and the others who truly saw me and offered a hand-up.

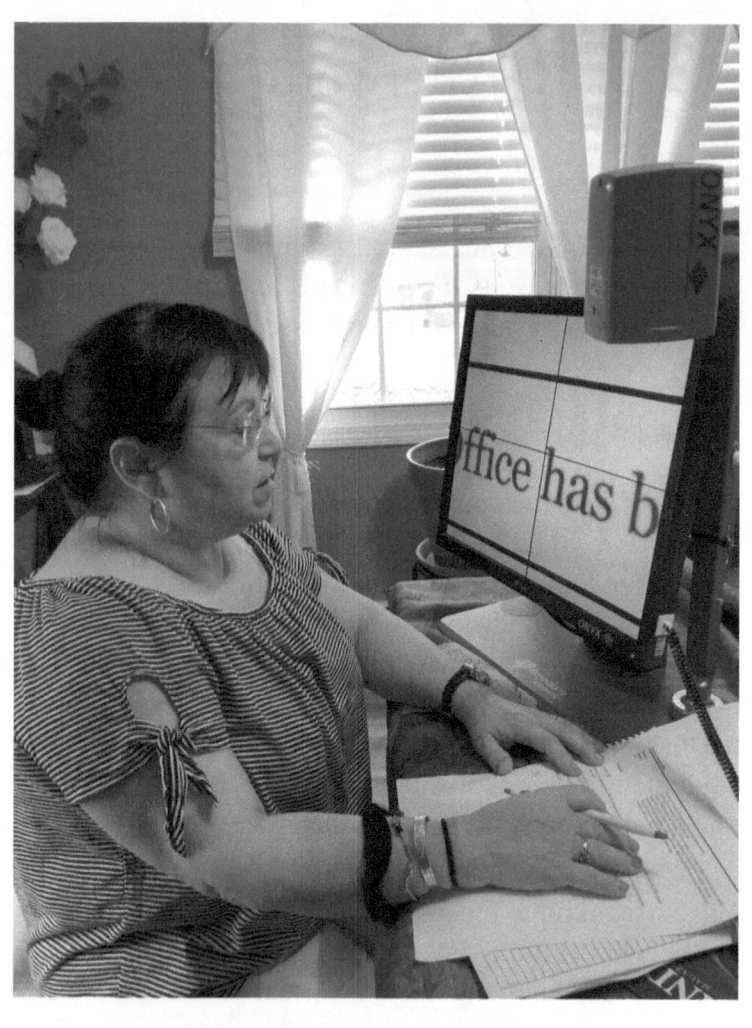

GIULIA USING HER ADAPTIVE READING EQUIPMENT

My "family" is a whole different thing these days, and everything I missed as a kid is here for me now. For the first time, I have friends who unselfishly support me. When I started writing this book, Jake and Carolyn came and helped me type. My husband would read me the stories in bed. All of this helped create a special connection between me, my husband Dan, and my sons Jake and Luke. We have an incredible bond! Luke kept me grounded by always being there making sure I did what I needed to do. My husband corrected my spelling, and Jake and Luke added their love to the mix.

I am eternally grateful for my husband Dan. We learned about life as a team, went to college together, and found our careers at the same time. Dan became a cop while I continued to work towards my degree, and we had two beautiful boys. This book may not seem like a love story, but to me, all of my trials and trauma disappear when I'm with my team. My boys walk to the store together with me, and I marvel at my new world.

I have FREEDOM, I can be me...with no judgment. My kids are ambassadors of love and support, and my husband loves me. My girlfriends' kids will drive me if I'm stuck for a ride. I love my job, and my clients remain my passion.

The ghosts of the past no longer haunt me. Believe me, my memories aren't gone—but they no longer carry the same the painful sting.

Observe your story, learn the lesson, and focus on today. Fit into your skin, focus on your happiness, and live your new story with energy and determination. Remember: *If it's to be, it's up to me.*

Make active gratitude a part of your daily practice. In my case, everyone did the best they could, even though their actions at the time were pretty deplorable. Now I know that nothing was personal...Not one thing—and every experience helped bring me to where I am today.

I am grateful for my amazing life, my husband, friends, kids and now, even my parents. By forgiving them, and shifting my anger to gratitude, I have freed myself to live and thrive in my world—on my terms.

Hey, if I can do it, so can you. Whatever your circumstances, you, too, can Navigate in the Darkness, find YOUR light, and shift into positivity.

I'm cheering you on! Hurray!!

Acknowledgments

Lillian Poston: My dearest Lillian, no words can possibly describe how I feel about you and how much I want to thank you. I met you at one of the lowest points in my life. The minute I looked in your eyes the warm energy was magical. You accepted me, as you do to all, with love and unconditional regard. The more you taught me, the more I wanted to know. Your wisdom is beyond words. You shared all that I asked for and more. You are the angel that taught me how to navigate through life. You made me feel as if I was one of your own children. Most of all, you gave me my soul—literally and figuratively. Ho'oponopono!

Raven DiMario: You have always made me feel like I could touch the stars. No matter what we discussed, you always made me feel like a woman with great potential and capacities. Each time we talk I feel as if I can touch the moon. You always have kind words to share and make the glass l have full. You have a tremendous way of letting people feel comfortable and accepted unconditionally. For that I am grateful...as well as for all the wonderful food we shared together and all the recipes you taught me. Your love of art and food has made me see the world in a better light. Thank you for painting the beautiful sunflower for me when I first opened my private practice. It brings a smile too many people's faces, including mine.

Heather McNeil: Thank you for being there for me. You have always stood by me throughout my journey. When I was afraid, I knew all I needed to do was call you and my fears would disappear. You help me stay strong and gave me guidance at every turn, in every corner, and in each battle. You have always accepted me and had faith in me even when I had no faith in myself. No words can express how much you mean to me as a friend, a mentor and as one of my angels. Thank you for the unconditional care and love you have always shown me. I look forward to our continuing journey.

Michael Berk: Thank you for treating me with respect and dignity, and for being a rock of truth for me. You have helped me to see the world in a way that made it less scary. Just when I thought I had hit a wall you were always there to help me see that the wall was just another pebble. You have helped me see that being different is a strength and being bright is not a curse. You thought that walking tall and carrying a big white stick is truly a good thing! You are a pillar of strength and courage. Thank you for sharing all your truth and wisdom—I am a better human being for it. You have always been there to help me with anything I needed with useful advice, and you never treated me like I was never a bother—even when I felt like I was. Thank you for being my brother.

ACKNOWLEDGMENTS

Carolyn Perez: Thank you for all the long days and nights you spent reading my books to me, being my typist, my personal driver, my babysitter, and my confidant. Thank you for loving me, my boys and my husband with all your heart and soul. You have done so much for me and my family without asking for anything in return. I never knew what unconditional love from a friend meant and felt like until I met you. I can't even begin to think where my life would be without you taking me into your life. No words I can say will ever be able to capture the amount of gratitude and love I have for you. I look forward to many more years of friendship.

My husband Daniel: Thank you for being by my side, as my typist, my taxi, my confidant, my partner, and all the other roles you have played in our life together. You have been there for me through thick and thin and through good and bad. You have always allowed me to be whoever I wanted to be. You gave me the freedom to be my own person in spite of it all. With you, I have always felt the freedom to express myself and have had my needs met. You have sacrificed for me and rescued me when I needed it. Without your love and support, I wouldn't be the person I am today. I am truly blessed and look forward to continuing our life adventure together.

My sons Jacob and Lucas: I am so blessed to have both of you in my life. Due to my vision problems, I feel that there were responsibilities that fell to both of you that were not always fair. You both had to grow up prematurely, and I sometimes feel that you missed out on some of the childhood events that I was unable to provide, such as reading you a bedtime story or driving you to little league game and watching you play, or seeing you perform really well in Karate. My heart ached because I couldn't see if someone was picking on you. I couldn't see to cheer for you or defend you. Both of you sacrificed your own time outside or playing video games so you could help me. Thank you for who you are and everything you have done for me. Mostly, I want to tell you how lucky I feel that you love me and are my boys. The world is a better place because you are in it. Bringing each of you into this world is the BEST thing I have ever done.

Stewart Cohen: My beautiful friend and mentor! I am so thankful for the thoughtfulness and love you gave me. Even though you acted tough, I got to know the real you. You were supportive, kind, loving, generous, and knew exactly when I needed the extra push to do the right thing for my future. Fear was not allowed in your life and you made sure it did not lead me. I am grateful for the countless words of wisdom and the fatherly talks you had with me and my husband Dan. Because of you, I was nominated and received a top alumni award, and was asked by professors to speak in their classes. Because of you, I am the person I am today in my professional life. I will always be forever grateful to you and I am so sorry that you were taken from this earth way too soon. We really needed to talk a lot more. I miss you with all my heart and soul.

About the Author
GIULIA JARAMILLO, MS, LMFT

Giulia Jaramillo was born in Italy and emigrated with her parents to the United States in 1968. Her first diagnosis of Macular Degeneration came in 1971. Her education includes graduating from Westerly High and Cosmetology School, as well as a Bachelor of Science degree from the University of Rhode Island, where she graduated *summa cum laude* in 2001. She furthered her studies with a Master of Science degree in Marital and family therapy, thereby establishing her shoreline, Connecticut psychotherapy practice that she continues today.

Her knowledge includes various techniques such as Reiki, Mindfulness, and other non-traditional modalities, and she has treated patients with anxiety, depression, trauma, and the ravages of PTSD. She works with disabled individuals, couples, families in crisis, and regularly supports the Court Support Services Division in court cases.

Her family remains Giulia's primary focus. She and her husband Dan live close by to their two beloved grown sons. Together, they are dedicated to serving their community without judgment or prejudice.

Connect with Giulia at gjaramillo@gmail.com or 860-333-2411

Resources

Books:

The New Earth by Eckhart Tolle
The Power of Now by Eckhart Tolle
Life Visioning by Michael Bernard Beckwith
The Four Agreements by Don Miguel Ruiz
The Alchemist by Paulo Coelho
The Secret by Rhonda Byrne
You Can Heal Your Life by Louise Hay
Mindfulness by Joseph Campbell
Remarkable Adults by Stewart Cohn

Department of Rehabilitation Services—Also known as DORS or Bureau of Vocational Rehabilitation Services. They help with all kind of documented disabilities.

Library of the Blind and Dyslexia—Has all books on tape. If it is in their library, they will put it on tape for you.

Maxi Aids—Adaptive equipment for the visual and hearing impaired.

www.Tigers.com—Adaptive equipment of all kinds.

Vision Dynamics, Shelton CT.—Adaptive equipment for the blind; provides hands-on training for all of their products.

New England Low Vision and Blindness, New Britain, CT.

South East Center of the Blind, New London, CT.

Center for the Blind—Locations in each state.

Eastern CT Transportation Consortium—They are part of SEAT and will pick you up at your home.

Additional Books by Flower of Life Press

The Caregiving Journey: Information. Guidance. Inspiration.

The New Feminine Evolutionary:
Embody Presence—Become the Change

Pioneering the Path to Prosperity: Discover the Power of True Wealth and Abundance

Emerge: 7 Steps to Transformation
(No matter what life throws at you!)

Practice: Wisdom from the Downward Dog

Sacred Body Wisdom: Igniting the Flame of Our
DIvine Humanity

Sisterhood of the Mindful Goddess: How to Remove Obstacles, Activate Your Gifts, and Become Your Own Superhero

Path of the Priestess: Discover Your Divine Purpose

Sacred Call of the Ancient Priestess:
Birthing a New Feminine Archetype

Rise Above: Free Your Mind—One Brushstroke at a Time

Menopause Mavens: Master the Mystery of Menopause

The Power of Essential Oils: Create Positive Transformation in Your Well-Being, Business, and Life

Self-Made Wellionaire: Get Off Your Ass(et), Reclaim Your Health, and Feel Like a Million Bucks

Oms From the Heart: Open Your Heart to the Power of Yoga

The Four Tenets of Love:
Open, Activate, and Inspire Your Life's Path

The Fire-Driven Life:
Ignite the Fire of Self-Worth, Health, and
Happiness with a Plant-Based Diet

Visit us at **www.FlowerofLifepress.com**

www.ingramcontent.com/pod-product-compliance
Lightning Source LLC
Chambersburg PA
CBHW030328080526
44584CB00012B/765